The Numbers Game

Viora Mayobo

authorHOUSE

AuthorHouse™
1663 Liberty Drive
Bloomington, IN 47403
www.authorhouse.com
Phone: 1 (800) 839-8640

Published by AuthorHouse   03/08/2016

ISBN: 978-1-5049-6136-3 (sc)
ISBN: 978-1-5049-6137-0 (e)

Print information available on the last page.

I dedicate this book to the multitudes of people out there, who barely have a life to live. The world economy has gone haywire, leaving many with no place to start. Everything people thought they knew changed in an instant when the economy of the world went south in 2008. People's retirement savings were wiped out in a flash. But that has come and gone. Ready yourselves for what is yet to come… the unforeseen future.

Contents

I would like to thank my father... for not allowing his old age to prohibit him from doing what he really loved -to care for his children. Father still walked hundreds of miles at seventy eight, in search of ways to provide for his family.

Although we didn't have much growing up, father gave us reason to believe all circumstances were temporary, and that nothing is permanent. Father gave us all the love and attention we needed to stay focused, and the courage to keep pushing forward, even when nothing seemed possible... at the time. Father also told us to keep trying so long as time permits.

Introduction

I worked tirelessly from the get go – work hard, make lots of money, and go back home. Even with not much to show for I still believed anything was possible here in the land of opportunity. But when the job I thought was secure evaporated from my grasp like one very cold winter morning, I was left to wonder...what now? I prayed for a better paying job and hoped for change to come soon. Unfortunately, that job or day never showed, at least not in time to save the day. With bills pilling up faster than my brains could process information, I was getting desperate, and had good reason to be – I didn't want to loose all I already had. I remember thinking so hard, scouring my little brains for answers. But when nothing made sense, I was willing to settle; I started looking for anything, and that's exactly what I got ...anything.

The Numbers Game Merged

Have you ever wondered why we live by the numbers? Let me rephrase that question to make you understand what I mean: Why are numbers so important to us? The answer to this question is quite simple. Numbers allow us to position ourselves in our society; they tell us where we belong. If you have fewer numbers or none at all, then you undoubtedly make yourself believe you belong in the *P quadrant*.

For example, people in our society have a tendency of weighing others dependent upon where they live, the size of their house, the type of car they drive, the position they hold, the clothes they wear, the thickness of their degree, etc.

What exactly is the P quadrant? The P quadrant is where the poor belong. Why? The answer is simple: Their numbers don't amount to much of anything. If you are poor, then you will perhaps spend more time struggling than you will living. You go to bed at night not knowing where to start on the following day, and because of that simple fact, you fall prey to the numbers game and you become a statistic.

Before I go into further detail, please allow me to introduce myself to you. My name is Viora Mayobo. I was born in a small town of Mumbwa, in Central Province, Zambia, Southern Africa.

Zambia is a landlocked country, completely surrounded by other countries. There are no visible seas or oceans in this beautiful country, but certainly harbors a great deal of compound landscapes, including valleys, lakes, rivers, man-made dams, the Victoria Falls, and more, all mounted on every angle of every corner of its boundaries, most of which offer famous tourist attractions.

Father worked as first secretary to the governor in our small township, Mumbwa, for many years. When father decided to retire, and with no other options from which to choose, we moved to the village. The change was sudden and intimidating to us... the children.

Within a short period of time, we went from being kids to full-blown farmers. Farming was not only hard but complicated as well. Although we had a tractor and other modern farming equipment, most of the work had to be done manually. For example, the planter would plant seeds, and we would run behind to make sure seeds lined up properly. By the day's end, we would be good for nothing but sleep.

In the village a normal day begins early in the morning, usually before dawn. Every morning, we went to the farm to cultivate the land, to grow crops for profit. Everything we did from that point on revolved around farming. We woke up before dawn, in most instances as early as four o'clock, to go to the farm across the river. We spent the whole day working the land: Planting seeds, weeding, and keeping monkeys away from crops. We went home after dark, when monkeys went to sleep. This was soon to become our way of life for years to come.

Moving from our small township to the village was quite a change. We left behind everything we loved and cherished – schools, friends, and neighborhoods, to which we were accustomed. As is usually the case with most children, we complained, talked about anything and everything, and sometimes just stared into space with frustration ...wondering what was to come next. But as days turned into weeks, and months into years, our memories slowly began to fade away, though occasionally we would revisit our memories here and there. At last the hard truth took hold.

Change is never easy; regardless of the circumstances, change can be as intimidating as it is uncertain. Everything we were used to before relocating quickly became history. Village life was somehow confusing though, and a lot of things did not make any sense to me or my siblings. Access to water, for instance, was miles away from home, for firewood one had to walk another few miles away from the village.

My father was very old when he started having children. As a result, he was unable to adequately support us financially through school. The only thing my father really cared about was education. Although at the time I was just a child and didn't know any better, I sometimes questioned his judgment.

At other times I thought he hated us because there were too many of us. What I did not realize was that all he ever wanted was the best for us. I didn't understand that, because my brains were still forming and I was not grown enough to fully comprehend his intentions.

Education

When we moved to the village, we walked three and a half hours every morning to go to school and then another three and a half to go back home. As horrible and unbelievable as this may sound, it was something we had to do if we were to make something of ourselves. The excruciating pain of having to walk or run to school for hours were concessions with which we were inclined to live for years to come.

After years of trying to adapt to the new system, we finally got used to it. We became stronger and smarter than all the other children who had the luxury to choose how they went to school. Perhaps most surprising was how my brothers and sisters became school-oriented; we put our education above all else, pouring our souls into it, as failure was not a luxury any of us could afford.

But shortly after going to secondary school, an unfortunate pattern emerged. If we had money to buy books, then we were short on something else of equal importance. This quickly took a toll on some of us. After going through a sequence of repeated circumstances, a problem that started out small turned into an unimaginable reality. This forced some of us to grow up too soon. We grew up in a hurry …so we could care for our younger siblings; we turned to the one thing we could do to raise money for their school. We started selling men's shoes and dried fish.

Aspirations

While in the village, as one of my sisters and I walked to a nearby river in the evening to draw drinking water, we heard a sound from a distance. That sound turned out to be noise from an airplane. And as the noise drew closer and louder, I looked up and saw a plane flying right above us. The noise was so tempting.

My sister and I stood still for a few seconds, looking in the direction of where the airplane was headed. I remember telling my sister, Beauty, how I wished the plane could take me with it. Where I ended up was not much of a concern of mine, as long as I didn't have to live in the village another day.

I was a much younger girl at the time, but even then I already knew I wasn't going to be spending the rest of my life in the village. Everything people in the village did on a daily basis, played to my weakness. Although I had no idea how I was going to leave home, the unforeseen future was beginning to develop.

Our means were limited, and I was very much aware of that fact. However, leaving the village wasn't something I was about to let anybody convince me of otherwise. Change was inevitable.

After the noise from the plane faded away, I began to realize that there was more to life than meets the eye. I spent the entire week imagining myself flying out of the country, Zambia. This happened at a time when the word "fantasy" felt hollow; it was a word that carried no meaning of any sort to me. But I was determined to acquire my goal through any means possible.

Being forever enslaved by village living was something I never envisioned for myself. While we didn't have much growing up, I also realized that was in my past. It was not associated with where I ended up. And I wasn't about to let my past define my future either.

Last Day of School

One winter morning after school closed, I said good-bye to all my friends, as though I was never going back. We hugged, we cried, and we held hands like there was no tomorrow. I had no idea I was seeing some, if not all of them, for the very last time.

I might not have known what belie ahead, but something within me subconsciously told me that was it. That event occurred at an interesting moment when access to my own instincts was next to none. I knew little about the word "instinct," which makes me believe the thought was a perfectly calculated coincidence, because none of us went back to the village after that.

I went to the home of my sisters who lived in Lusaka, the capital of Zambia. And because she did not have financial stability, I immediately hit the ground running. I had no doubt in my mind that successful people possessed unique characteristics that most unsuccessful people did not. I knew that the only way out of our current situations was digging in the mud for possibilities.

Without question, there's too great of a risk in going into any business, regardless of its nature, without a well-defined plan. But I thought I would be better suited with a loss than to not try at all. I would rather fail than sit idly by waiting for nothing.

Young as I was, I knew that the only distinction that could be drawn between successful people and those who are not was the motivation to try. Die trying, or live with the agony of terror that comes along with not knowing what's next. The terror of being afraid of your own shadow becomes inexplicably clear.

Quite often, we seek out easy ways; in other words, we slave away for nothing, for fear of the unknown. As a last resort, we turn to self-defeating practices of doing little or nothing at all, which in most cases keep us from realizing our true potential.

Life after School

Because money was not in abundance, some of us chose to home-school. By now, our father had become our dependent, as he was too old to do anything. We worked hard to ensure he had everything he needed in the village. One of us would visit him in the village every once in a while.

In the late 1980s, Father lived in a village where there were no phones. The only way we communicated with him and everybody in the village was by handwritten letters or word of mouth. Regular mail, at that time, took anywhere from two weeks to a month to make it to its destination.

Communication in this corner of the world, to this day, is an industrial problem. People who still live in this part of the world climb in trees to speak on their cell phones. This is because they receive better signals in trees than when standing on level ground. People would much rather climb trees to communicate than be left behind or cut off from the rest of the world. Great strides have since been made in terms of technology, yet still, not much has changed in that part of the world.

I know that some of you who know nothing about life in the village will find this rather interesting and intriguing all at once. Why? For the simple fact that we live in the twenty-first century, when technology is at its peak, yet we still have a good chunk of people in remote parts of the world lagging behind. One can only imagine how life in these parts of the world is really like.

In these remote villages, life consists of organic food, traditional medicine or herbs, water drawn from a nearby river or well (which was built in the 1600s). Civilization has come a long way, but all the while, people in remote corners of the earth have been forgotten.

People in these parts of the world do not have a need for doctors, and yet most live well past a hundred. If you are asking how that could be, you need to know that people in remote corners of the world have not been exposed to free medicines and free foods from the so-called industrialized world. Free medicines and free foods usually come at a hidden price. We can readily agree that nothing comes at no cost to anyone.

By the beginning of 1990, our father was seventy-eight, and his health was failing. On January 20, 1990, he passed away in his house, with his two sisters by his side. Our father had been sick for a short while and had been in and out of the hospital. Within the same time frame he contracted malaria, which would later end his life as we know it. He was laid to rest at the edge of the village, Chitapu.

Our father did so much for us. The only way to honor his memory is to keep his purpose alive, which is to never stop trying so long as time permits. Although my father would have preferred I be a nurse, writing wouldn't have been that much of a problem to him either.

Before Father died, he wanted me to marry a son of a very wealthy man in a nearby village. He asked for twelve herds of cattle as a form of payment for my marriage.

This was to be kept a secret; only elders in the village knew of it. But Mother made a mistake and said something that tipped me off. I immediately ran to my mother's, where I remained for three months until my father decided not to proceed with the plan.

When I came home, I told my father how I hated the idea of marrying someone from the village. We laughed about it for a while, and that was the end of the story. I went on with my life as if nothing had happened.

However, it is important to know that I didn't run from home because I hated the young and handsome man who wanted to marry me; I took off because spending my entire life in the village was not one of my motivations. Village life wasn't a foreseeable future I envisioned for thyself. And because I knew there was more to life than the norm of village life, I ran.

Getting married in the village meant becoming something you are not in order to fit in. But if the cattle had exchanged hands, there was nothing humanly possible I could have done to prohibit the marriage from taking hold.

This custom was a turnoff for me. I might not have known much about marriage in my teenage years, but knew a thing or two about it. I saw many demeaning things done to submissive, decent wives: The beating, the shouting, mockery, etc. And could not see myself living with that.

Father harbored our very best interest at heart. He always wanted the best for all of us. He committed the later part of his life doing the best that he could to ensure our needs were met, not his own. He was determined to provide for his family by any means dimmed necessary.

At age seventy eight, father still walked long distances in search of food. He woke up very early in the morning to go to the farm, like everyone else. Father wanted to think his age was just a number and not a disability.

Father had no known illnesses at seventy-eight; he was very strong and healthy. He never took any medication. For a headache he chewed bitter leaves, chewed the same leaves for a tummy ache.

Father was very well educated and well spoken. He really knew what he knew. He was one of the very few chosen ones from his village who made something of themselves, despite the fact that he was a stepchild.

His father died young, leaving his poor mother to care for three young children, my father and his two sisters. My grandmother remarried because she had no means to care for her little ones. She married my grandfather's brother, with whom she would have two sons.

You must by now wonder why I haven't said a word about mother. Mother was a full-time housewife who didn't have much to go on as it pertains to decision making. My father did everything. Mother was responsible for the budget. She ensured our household had adequate supplies for the whole family. She spent most of her time cooking, cleaning, and washing clothes by hand at a nearby stream—the good old-fashioned way!

Our maternal grandmother lived with us for a long time. She told us many things in our teenage years. She always told us not to marry men who talked too much. "You will spend most of your time arguing about foolish things," she said. Most of what she told us that many years ago still holds true today, long after she's been gone. As my grandmother had indicated, getting married to a man who talks too much would make you spend most of your time together pulling on each other, never agreeing on anything, which to me is a complete waste of time.

When my mother left our old father, he spent most of his time caring for our three little brothers. When he couldn't do it by himself any longer, he married his uncle's wife, who by the way took very good care of us ...as if we were her own.

I spent more of my teenage years with her than I did with Mother. She was there for us when we needed her most. She poured her soul into giving us her undivided attention we so desperately desired.

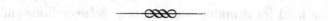

Coming to America

Our childhood was full of dreams and aspirations. We always wanted to go that extra mile when everyone else thought it was a gamble. We were no stranger to risk taking. We always wanted to do what no person thought was possible.

Coming to America was no different; it was gambling at its best! When we told our inner circles we were coming to America, that quickly became talk of the century, because they knew we had no known being who would be inclined take us in.

To live in one of the remotest corners of the world is probably the best part of being human; to experience life on different sides of the hemisphere is an opportunity only available to few. Perhaps the most surprising is the striking resemblance of how things ought to be done in different parts of the world.

Things are done one way or the other – you are either educated or you are not; either you know or you don't, either you work for another being or you work for yourself. Life in America and beyond the boarders is almost uniform; in order to have a life, one must work hard or he is homeless and ceases to exist.

In civilized countries, nobody has to go digging in the mud for drinking water or play *kalambe* (hide-and-seek) with monkeys in the nearby bushes when fetching for firewood. Still, things are done in pairs, one way or the other. Either you go to work and work hard or you are homeless and without a place to belong.

To this day, this debate rages on, people across the globe still don't understand that there are only two ways of doing things: You either do it the right way or the wrong way; you belong in one group of people or the other; either you get it or you don't—there's no middle ground. There's no such thing as the poor, the middle class, and the rich. You are either rich or you are poor—period!

The Difference in Culture

In some parts of the world a man is considered head of the household. While a lot has changed, it is still the man's responsibility to ensure the family is well taken care of. In some civilized countries, however, things don't work as such. In some homes the woman assume the responsibilities for both the man and that of the woman, and they do just fine.

This belief system, in my opinion, is one that favors men more than women, because in most instances, men want to have it both ways. What men fail to understand is that certain things are not to be confused. Carrying a pregnancy to term, for example, is a woman's responsibility. This is the very reason a man is to pay his wife's parents to marry their daughter. I, for one, know that I'm not for sale, neither am I for free.

There's no such thing as free, pay or don't bother with me. Like most women, I can be without a man and do okay, but every man needs a woman, unless he's impotent. And today there's a solution for that too. We have seen men turn into women for whatever reason.

With all these changes made over the years, men still spend a fortune on prostitutes... which leads me to believe a woman has no substitute. A woman holds the cards necessarily for the completion of the puzzle, including childbearing. Without a woman, there's no us – the entire world would otherwise be filled with nothing but clones.

If God didn't think a woman would be of great importance, he probably would have created Adam and Noah instead. Then what? Well, nothing! None of us would exist to ask those questions. Curiosity might not have existed otherwise.

No woman, no world! Or perhaps aliens might have continued to live on earth peacefully—no greed, no wars, no divisions, no racism, no lies, no betrayal, no jealousy, no killing, no money, no power, and so on. Without all these unsatisfying, never-ending evil desires, the world could be a much better place than what it is today, where everyone is at odds with everyone else.

Most men cheat because they've had too much of their wives for free. As a result, they turn to prostitutes for immediate gratification. No money, no sex—simple! If a mistress drives around in a Porsche for the same thing I can do, then why would I, as a housewife, drive around in a beat-up Toyota Corolla? Getting paid to do something feels great! Stars with tons of money do it. Why don't you?

I know for sure that there's been a lot of debate about equality in some civilized countries, especially the fifty-fifty equation, but at what expense? The notion that men and women are equal is just pure madness. Man is to husband as woman is to wife; a household cannot be run in a proper manner if both man and woman are considered equals. Gay/lesbian couples are no exception.

Most people in civilized countries have a tendency to think that women who depend on men for everything are somehow primitive or ignorant. No, they are not. They just have a different culture, one that allows a man to take care of his wife and children. And by the way, most women in today's world are working mothers, wives, which explains why most marriages are on life support? Woman's contributions to households is one thing, taking care of old, broke-ass fools is another.

In some countries the man will be responsible for rent, school fees for the children, family health insurance, savings, car notes, auto insurance, food, and clothing. The woman will be responsible for the rest: electricity, cable, phone, and so on. This might sound like an error, but most people can readily agree that a man gains respect when he takes good care of his family.

It is fine to disagree here. But what you must understand is that your husband is not yours alone, and therefore, are not inclined to take care of him. Most likely, whatever he doesn't do for you, he does for his mistresses, since you are superwoman with no needs. The mistress has needs and therefore gets the most attention from your husband, while you go around playing Grandmother.

Your husband is neither your brother nor your father, and you can argue with me until doomsday if you would like. The fact stays the same. You have to be demanding in order to get the attention you deserve, before the other woman gets in between.

Believe it or not, the squeaky wheel gets the oil! Therefore, it is up to you to lay the ground rules and tell your hubby what you want. Either you keep pretending to be the civilized superwoman, or you claim your worth. If you haven't noticed already, men like rough women. The cards are yours to play, or be cheated.

Men are not bound by their own words or actions. Almost all men, at one point or another, deceive with every chance that comes their way. The same has proved to be true, of even less certainly suspected figures. Men who seem to be devoted husbands cheat also. You can keep telling yourself what you want to believe, but it is what it is—a game.

A long time ago, it was a man's job to approach a woman, but even that less sophisticated matter has changed with time. Today, most women do not have the patience to wait to be approached. They go out of their way to find what they identify as true love.

In a few weeks it's over, and they are on to the next thing. Why? It's because women are so desperate for love. I'm in my second quarter of life, yet I've never had the stamina to chase after men. It's ugly out there!

Domestic Violence

Domestic violence is one of the root causes of broken homes in America and around the globe. And when families get ripped apart, in most instances, the mother is left alone to care for the little ones. In very rare circumstances will the little ones be left under the care of the father. This is because most men don't want to be burdened. But with the mother it's just the opposite.

Some men even go into hiding to avoid child support. And I speak from experience, not speculation. Some men don't seem to understand that taking care of children is the responsibility that of both the mother and the father; they tend to think they do have the luxury to pick and choose what he can and can not do.

I have come to realize that there no rules strong enough to protect the well being of our children in today's world. Simply because most of us think that taking care of children is the responsibility only of the parents, when in fact we all are involved one or the other way; we are brother's keeper.

I know also that most men put themselves above all else, including taking care of their own children. I would have loved to see more done to redress the issue at hand. But unfortunately, we live in a world with uneven grounds, where some are allowed to do as they please.

Everyone has his/her own interpretations of things, which leads me to believe laws if any are broken. We have heard loud talk, but not good enough to address any situations, or even provoke a change. It's almost as if your problems are yours alone to worry about, even if there are small children involved. We live in a wasteful planet where everything goes, even if it endangers the very livelihood of humanity.

Every year, I'm asked to refile my taxes and provide proof of my children being under my care the whole tax season. This pattern presents a much larger problem to me and my kids than just taxes. If I'm not being audited by the IRS, then I don't receive any money back at all. I can only wish something could be done to ensure some people were not being rewarded for their cowardly behavior, for claiming children with whom they have no relationship.

We all know that claiming children who are not under your care as your dependents is not only wrong but a punishable crime as well. Allowing certain caricatures to file their taxes and claim children with whom they have no relationship, speaks to the brokenness of world systems. I honestly don't know why nobody does anything, or ask questions. People have to know that your children don't automatically qualify as your dependents if you are not taking care of them. Having children does not necessarily mean they are your dependents.

I find it extremely troubling to realize that nobody has any interest in resolving simple problems such as finding those running from taking care of their own children, especially when there are innocent children involved. Minor children are the responsibility of their parents—both parents, not just the mother or the father.

Over the years, most people have wondered why majority of people all around the world prefer to spend more money on Mother's Day than on Father's Day. What those wondering have also failed to realize is that mothers carry the pregnancy to term. Nine months is a very long time to carry through, and children know that.

While this assumption might appear biased to some, it actually is true. The bond that exists between mothers and their children is one that is unbreakable. And my trajectory here is not to suggest fathers do not play a role in their children's lives, because some of them do... The number of responsible fathers who honestly care about the well being of their children does account for a very small fraction, and that... I know for sure.

I have lived in many places because of circumstances far beyond my control. And because of that, I have seen the bad, the ugly, the worst of humanity. Certain things I cannot explain. What I do know also is that domestic violence is the prime reason most women and their children end up on the street.

Some people have no regard to human life. Although there are two sides to every story, I do understand also that I am only responsible for my narrative.... and can say anything I want about what I know and believe to be true.

I have met many women in my pursuit of life, each with a four T – a tall tale to tell. Those with a weak mind have ended up in psychiatric wards, some on 24/7 suicide watch, yet not one person seems to pay any attention to what is happening. All these women and children are collateral damage... they will be devoured before anyone takes notice.

When family tag-of-war begins, most men, as is the case with many fathers, dust their butts off, run as fast as they can. And their children's well being becomes secondary. My kids and I became homeless, yes, because of domestic violence. But the main reason that led up to homelessness was a different one. My kids and I became homeless because I couldn't work. I couldn't work because I had to take orders to survive, and staying home was one of them.

Spending nights in unfamiliar territory accelerated my aging process. I spent hours trying to make myself feel better; I spent other times looking for answers to the many questions that occupied my little brains.

Everything I did, including whom I made friends with, was monitored. And that made me look older than my maternal grandmother at 89; after that some would say... "look at you! Don't take the kids with you if you want to leave; I will hunt you down and cut you to pieces if you do." "I'm sure by now you know that nobody cares about you," they added.

One morning, my younger son didn't feel very well, so I asked him to stay home from school. And that quickly became a problem, one I never saw coming.

Making decisions involving my children was becoming an issue, but, motherhood is a position no one can take away from me. If there is one thing I am not willing, over my dead body, to surrender, it the care of my children. There's no person large enough to make me give up my motherly stance; my children are my responsibility, even in a foreign land.

Never in a million years did I ever realize I was going to be the one fighting for my position in life. When that time did come, I knew how to fight with tooth and nail, about every problem. I learned to push back, hard, if pushed. I didn't let anyone reduce my value for any reason.

I also learned to fight for my children. Protecting my children was something I was determined to do at every cost, even if it means I become homeless.

As all that was happening, I was busy trying to figure out how to leave. I quietly started building my exit strategy. I talked to close friends... who suggested I take out a restraining order.

Sometime in August, 2011... I went to Fulton County Superior Court to face a judge and to express my fears. When the judge asked me what I want done. I said I was afraid of the person, and that I wanted him to leave the house.

The judge granted my request and sent a sheriff to our apartment to serve the other person with a restraining order, but ... wasn't there. The following day, another sheriff made multiple attempts, but the person wasn't there. One of the sheriffs then notified some of their colleagues who also lived at Park Towers, where we lived, and asked them to keep a close eye at our door.

I had no idea how law enforcement took it to heart to protect victims of domestic violence until I was one myself. Every day, different sheriffs came to our door to check on us. When they couldn't serve the person, they went to the leasing office to ask management to deactivate his key card. They also asked property security to watch out for him.

The guard on duty came to our door to ask for a picture of my family. Around 3:00 AM., cameras captured the person trying to sneak in through the back entrance. Park Towers had security cameras mounted on every corner of the building, and one of the cameras picked up the stranger. He stood there for a long while trying to open the gate. When he failed to open the gate, he left hurriedly.

First thing in the morning, I received a call from the stranger, asking me why the key card was deactivated. I told him to direct that question to the property manager, who later told me that he called and was asked to call Sandy Springs Police.

After that, the trail of the stranger went cold. Our rent was not paid, and our electricity was turned off for nonpayment. My kids used candles to do their homework. We lived in the dark and bathed in cold water for two weeks before we left for Missouri.

Our good neighbor cooked food for us until we finally left. Looking back, I don't know if I could have done something any differently.

I come from a family that puts family values above all else. My father didn't have a problem taking care of my mother and her family. He never complained, even when things went far beyond his control, he took it like the head of the household.

Capitalizing on Unpleasant Circumstances

Believe it or not, opportunities did come of these horrible situations. I started looking for ways to make money, immediately. I became a very good freelance writer, something that would not have happened had I not chosen to step out of my comfort zone. I learned to fend for myself, something I had always wanted to do.

There's no better way to explain change. Although there are things we wish could stay the same forever, we must also begin to realize that sometimes change is inevitable. Sometimes change is about all that we need to break the cycle of domestic violence, the cycle of struggle.

In my pursuit of change, I've learned to make money reading e-mails, filling out forms, making a few phone calls, and so on. I really didn't make enough money doing all this, but it was just about what I needed to break loose and begin a new chapter in life.

I'm sure the stranger I left behind thought I wasn't going to make it without him; without him there was no me. What he miscalculated was the power of free will. I am free and delivered from bondage, the possessive behavior that led the stranger to believe without him there was no tomorrow.

Even as I try to reflect on past occurrences, I can't resist to ask why it took me eleven years to try, although a part of me kept telling me to hold tight because of my children, I still believe leaving was the best thing to do. Of course, there were numerous reasons I would have wanted to stay, but even more so by leaving. I wanted my children to grow up in a peaceful, quiet, and loving environment where they didn't have to protect me from aliens.

For months I kept at it. My plan to leave Atlanta, Georgia, had been in the making for years. I kept putting it off because of my boys. But when the effects of violence could no longer be concealed, even in the darkest corners of our own home, I knew that the time to go was past due. The decision only I could make had come, and there was nothing anyone could have said or done to prevent me from departing. Wherever we ended up wasn't much of a concern to me anymore, as separation had taken a firm grip of of my life.

I was going to be taking minor children with me. The exit plan had already been worked out. Although I knew a plan without money is the fools game, it was one that I was willing to die trying, because staying would only escalate tensions, turning a bad situation into a worse one.

After years of trying, I acknowledged I had, had enough. I finally decided to leave and never glance back. At the time, I really didn't have much of a choice besides became homeless. I had to rely mostly on my instincts and my faith that wherever we ended up, everything was going to be just fine. It doesn't take rocket science to realize that sometimes when we succumb to what is, we turn a blind eye to the very concept necessary for our survival, so to speak.

Many times, I felt belittled and hopeless. But knew that everything was going to be okay.

I refused to be taken apart piece by piece in front of my children. It would have been a very demeaning experience to have my kids see me cry.

The decision to leave turned out to be the best one I'd ever have to make in this life cycle. It opened up a whole new world of opportunities that wouldn't have otherwise been realized had I chosen to hang on.

Living with certain people under the same roof is a nightmare no human being should have to go through. Even after leaving, I consistently had to watch my back. Sometimes fibers in my whole body moved, indicating something horrible was about to happen to me.

Living in continuous fear accelerated my aging process. I slept with one eye open to see where the first punch was going to land, and it was at that point did I realize I had to go. And here I am, years after leaving, and I'm still trying to dissect the truth and wondering why.

I find myself trying to protrude the fact that it took me a while to take a stand; but sometimes time is what we need to get informed about certain situations.

Homelessness

Homelessness is not something anyone can have time to prepare for. Aside from uncertainty, homelessness brings along with it many unexpected twists and turns. But it was a risk I was all too willing to take after years of living under worst conditions any human being alive today could ever go through. Some people's cruelty made me realize just how good of a choice homelessness was. It was better than having to spend another day or night under the same roof with those people.

I undoubtedly do realize most people would find that quite difficult to fathom, and I don't expect you to. All I want is that people know what happens when you fight with your own guts. I spent more than eleven years trying to convince myself it was going to be fine. One can only imagine why. Quite simply, it means I had nobody and nowhere to go. My alien status made for a perfect target for some. But that has since changed. I'm now able to live like a human being again, work wherever I want.

Certain persons know how to prey on their victims. They are very much acquainted with how the system works. They know how long it takes the police to show up once a 911 call is placed. I was always reminded that a few seconds was all that was needed to destroy and disfigure me permanently, and I took very seriously every word produced.

After years of living in constant fear, I finally decided to take the bet. My every move was consistently monitored, accusing me of having relationships that never existed. Some people are very unpredictable and insecure; one minute they'd be laughing and kicking and shouting the next. I didn't know what to make of it.

The Hospital

Consequently, I wasn't allowed to speak to anyone, including my sisters. When I was in the hospital in 2006, I was gravely ill, yet even my sisters weren't allowed to visit; my sister Beauty wanted to fly in from Bowie, MD. to visit with me and help take care of the boys, but was told not worry about it.

I was so sick that I dreamed with my eyes open; a nurse came by the next morning to see how I was doing. When she said good morning, I smiled and looked her. She looked at me with the biggest smile I had seen in years and said to me "the doctors wondered if you were going to make it through the night". I realized at that point just how ill I was and how important it was that I appreciate life a little bit more.

That day, when my cousin came to the hospital with my two boys, I hugged them and kissed them as though the last. Although I was certain I wouldn't die that easily, I was still in pretty bad shape, and anything could tip the balance either way.

I didn't know what a great will to live was until I looked at myself in the mirror and failed to recognize myself. I had lost half of my being in just a few days. That was when I realized I had a great desire to live. I was afraid of never seeing my little ones again, so I did the one thing I had strength for—prayed. I prayed so I could live to see another dawn of day and my little boys.

The eleven days I spent in the hospital felt like a hundred. I didn't really worry much about dying; time for that would come for sure, which requires no permission from me, and would most likely do so when I least expect it? But the idea of leaving my two little boys in the care of the unknown kept me awake at night all night.

I had been sick for two weeks but kept masking the pain with Tylenol, because I didn't want my boys to live without me. One night I woke to this excruciating pain on one side of my chest. I couldn't turn, and I couldn't move or breathe. The pain got worse with every move I made. By 5:00 AM., I started gasping for air because the pain in my diaphragm was unbearable. It was unlike anything I could imagine.

I immediately asked to be taken to the hospital. Everyone we met along the way stared at us. The lady at the desk immediately called for a wheelchair. She asked if I had been involved in a car accident. Shaking my head was all I had strength for.

I was rushed to a room, and within a few minutes the whole room was filled with doctors. Some were taking my vitals, and others were monitoring my heart. There was so much commotion going on, but none of the doctors said much as they stared at one another.

I was in and out of consciousness quite a few times. I wasn't even aware of my surroundings. And couldn't distinguish dream from reality, day from night. Sometimes

I thought I was dreaming with my eyes open, and other times I was listening with my eyes closed, before the doctors finally determined I had pneumonia, and both of my lungs had collapsed.

Still at the edge of the darkest pit known to Mankind, I had no doubt in my wildest imagination that I was going to make it out alive. I'm not a doctor, but I'm no stranger to death either. Over the years, I have lost many of my loved ones, most of whom predicted their own deaths, whether they had been sick or died in a car accident, they all saw their own deaths. I hadn't seen mine, so I knew I had ways left to go.

As much as I wanted to live, begging for my life had not crossed my mind just yet. You can beg for your life to be spared, but if your time to go has come, no word will be good enough to prevent the inevitable - death. You might as well pray for the transition to be quick and smooth.

Moving to Missouri

When I set out to start a new life more than five years ago, nothing could have adequately prepared me for the magnitude of what was to come. Even with years of planning under my sleeve, I still was unable to ready myself for the occasion. In cases where my kids and I had to spend nights out in the cold at the Greyhound bus station, I was left with no words to describe my experiences.

I still remember feeling hopeless, with not much to go on, no money or a place to belong, it was surreal! The situation took an even surprising turn when our suitcases got stolen. We had about eight big suitcases, three of which were stolen in the early hours of one Sunday morning. That was just the beginning of what would come to be part of the many unexpected turns of events.

When my daughter's feet got swollen, they were the biggest I had ever seen. My daughter refused to lie down for two days. Because of lack of sleep and rest, my daughter's feet were dangerously inflated. I was left speechless, sleepless, and motionless. If this wasn't temptation, then I don't really know what is. I not only had to worry about where to go with my kids, but also feared the worst, losing a child while on the run. It doesn't get any worse than that, or so I thought.

You might not be able to resist the temptation to ask what I did as all these sad events unfolded. Well, please understand that I did nothing. "Why?" you may ask. Quite simply, I was not in a position to think or even do anything. My mind was overloaded, and my mouth was numb. All I did was stare into space, wondering, *What now?* Crazy was too good of a word! Homelessness became the most famous word in an instant.

Before I left home, sometime in 2011, I was very afraid to die. I wanted to be there for my kids, but after going through tough situations, I wondered where death was.

Immediately I thought, *Wait! Now that I'm left alone to pick up the pieces, I must begin to realize that nothing is permanent and everything is temporary. No matter how difficult things will be, we will be okay once all is said and done.* With that in mind I got up, dusted off, prepared myself for the obstacles that belie ahead, and kept going forward.

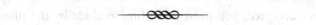

Life in Missouri

At dawn, everyone at the bus station—the sheriff, Greyhound employees, Good Samaritans, and everyone—took it upon themselves to take care of the problem at hand. Everyone was calling around, trying to find a place for me and my kids. That's when I realized just how caring and loving ordinary people we sometimes identify as strangers can be. Their immeasurable love and support came pouring in at a time when we needed it most. Complete strangers gave us coupons for free lunches and dinners.

Before noon, a break came! Personnel at a homeless shelter asked us to go for an intake at 3:00 PM. A lady, who was a Greyhound employee, told me to go immediately. When we got there, we were interviewed right away and given a place to stay.

This is where we were to spend a year. It wasn't the best of places, neither was it the worst. I loved the fact that I didn't have to be yelled at like a stepchild for no apparent reason. After years of living in a dungeon-like environment, I finally slept at peace—homeless but peaceful. Eleven years in a haunted home felt like a hundred.

In order to be accepted at the shelter, you must demonstrate that you need a place to start over. Case managers then assess your situation to determine eligibility. Once accepted, you must be willing to abide by the rules: Sign out every time you leave the building, and sign back in when you return.

Besides signing in and out, you also must attend weekly floor meetings and job search gatherings. If you fail to follow any of these rules, your case manager would talk to you. You have to exhibit good behavior to fit in.

Before then, I had an ill-conceived notion about homelessness—namely that homeless people were somehow stupid or lazy. It took me homelessness to understand why most people—good, hardworking people—become homeless.

Having gone through the worst experiences for an extended amount of time has made me think I owe it to myself to be happy and to be appreciative to be alive and well. It doesn't take a degree in rocket science to realize that our bodies are designed for happiness and joy. Even as I reflect on what happened to me and my kids in Atlanta, I never forget to forge a smile.

Doctors have repeatedly told us that it takes more muscles to flown than it takes to smile. Why then would one make thyself work harder to make good on evil, when you could work less and be happy. It's the numbers game. Do the math!

Today, I'm not afraid to be a number. To be honest, I'm not even good with numbers. Numbers to me are just... numbers!

Things that made me stay up all night don't move me an inch anymore. I have learned to persevere through it all. I try to focus all of my attention on positive thoughts. I've learned to take things one at a time. If my children are happy, I'm happy. Besides, I'm the happiest I've ever been. Life is too short to spend it worrying.

When people resort to desperate measures to find true love, all I say is "good luck with that!" Whether we like it or not, the world in which we live is strange and is constantly changing. This sometimes compensates for why human beings labor more than usual to keep up with the pace at which change occurs. Life is a game of chance. You can do all the right things and still mess up big-time. Life by the numbers!

At the shelter, a normal day begins very early in the morning. You have to be in the dining room by 7:00 AM if you want to eat breakfast. I didn't want to wake up my boys that early, so I had to come up with a way to make breakfast in my apartment. Apartments at the shelter come furnished; the only thing you won't find in these apartments is a stove.

So I learned to prepare eggs in a microwave for my children. I wanted to let my boys sleep in, especially on weekends. Everyday, I was reminded of how unpredictable life can be. But after a long time of sleepless nights in Georgia, I could finally sleep easy, knowing my kids and I were safe. There was no noise, no fighting, and no shouting.

I have learned to appreciate simple things I took for granted before we became homeless, such as being able to be a mother. Although I have developed a new set of skills in the process, I still feel as though I am the reason my kids have seen so much at such a young age. I have met good people in my pursuit of a better life.

The one thing we all had in common was the determination to find a way to financial independence. We never talked much with one another, because our minds were overwhelmed. My brains were in constant motion as I scoured them for solutions. When I felt like crying, I closed myself in the bathroom so my kids wouldn't see me cry. I always tried to maintain a positive attitude in front of my kids.

My kids asked me lots of questions, but mostly I had no answers: "Mommy, why did we leave home?" "When are we moving?" "When are you going to work?" "What is this place?" I had no easy answers to these questions. As a mother, I had to put on my best attitude and exhibit model behavior. Situations might have been far beyond the reach of my poor soul, but I was still a mother. I kept building on what was left of me, which was confidence.

Living in unstable environments feels like standing on shifting ground, where you have to constantly struggle to maintain balance. Life in the P quadrant is a game of chance; the outcome of everyday circumstances is unpredictable. Anything can tip the balance either way. Every day you are reminded of ugly truths around you.

To surrender your role as a parent and allow other people to dictate to you things you already know was perhaps the hardest challenge. You learn to survive, and pride becomes secondary.

Curfew begins at 9:00 PM. every evening, and all families are to remain in their apartments. If you are unable to make it home by 9:00 PM, you must have very good reason; otherwise you get sanctioned. More than three violations constitutes a strike, and you are asked to leave. In other words, your lease is terminated.

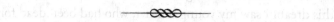

My Dearly Beloved Thelma

As if I hadn't been through enough already, on May 18, 2012, my dearly beloved daughter, who had been sick for a few months, died. I was on the phone the whole night with my elder sister and my son that night, who had been with her at the University Teaching Hospital in Lusaka, Zambia. By 6:00 AM., Zambian time (11:00 PM. in Kansas City, Missouri), I lost her. She was twenty-eight.

I didn't want to believe I was never going to see her again. I kept trying to convince myself it was just a bad dream, but it wasn't. It was one of those moments that leave you with no words for comfort.

Being homeless was hard, but losing a child was even harder. I didn't know what to make of it besides stare into space like a fool. The reality of losing a child is excruciatingly painful. All I did for more than three months was cry when the pain was unbearable. I felt alone and miserable. I wished it had never happened.

I cried day in and day out for three days. For three months, I sat there and thought about the day she was born. My memories of her were unmistakably clear in every aspect; her voice was so soft and sweet.

A day after my daughter's burial, I had a dream. In this dream I saw my young brother, who had been dead for years. He told me that he wanted to go with me to escort my daughter to her final resting place.

The three of us were suspended in midair as we floated around for hours. After flying for a few hours, my daughter and I crashed as we tried to land. I looked over to my brother, who was to my left, and asked if he had any idea why that happened. He hesitantly said my daughter and I crash-landed because I was angry. He then told me to let go of my anger so my daughter's soul could find a place of solace.

For months I kept thinking of that very strange dream and what it meant. I wanted to believe it was just a dream and that it would eventually fade away as time went by. But then, a few weeks after having that terrifying, vivid dream, I had yet another dream. This time my daughter appeared to me from a distance as I lay down. I wanted to kiss her so badly, but she just stood there, motionless. When I looked at her again, she was smiling. She looked very tall and pretty, as always, but before I could reach her, she slowly faded away.

Losing a child is a tribulation I will live with to the end of my days. I loved her with every fiber of my being. I wake up every day with her pretty face in my conscience, and I should. I wasn't there to touch her where it hurt the most.

When she died, every string of my soul wanted me to be there, but I couldn't for reasons far beyond my wildest imagination. Very quietly my tears pour down my old face in mourning. A chance to prove my motherhood to her is what will never come again.

There were times when I longed to see her again in my dreams, but when she did, she hardly said a word to me. She stared at me from a distance. In very rare circumstances would she speak to me in a language I didn't understand. It took me a while to fathom the message she was communicating to me. She wanted me to let go of my anger.

It's been four years since she moved on, yet every time I see her in my dreams, she leaves me hanging on to nothing but faith. For some reason, I don't have the fortitude to touch her when she stands close to me. "Why?" Is a question that will always linger in my small, bruised heart as I yearn for answers to this excruciating mystery!

I mentioned, however, that my kids and I were in Kansas City, Missouri, when my baby girl died. I was not only homeless but broke like a fool as well. When my daughter died, I reached out to our pastor at a church we went to while in Missouri. The pastor was rude enough to tell me that he was more interested in helping his daughter with her project than helping me bury my daughter.

Of course, I was disappointed with his response, given the fact that he was the pastor. I would have appreciated it if he had told me he didn't have the money. Being mean was absolutely uncalled for because I wasn't asking for much. But I also do realize it was his decision to make, not mine.

But because there are people out there who really care about others, money to bury my daughter became available just at the right time. My youngest daughter's friend's father went out of his way to wire money from his bank account

43

to mine late at night, in time for my little girl to receive a proper burial.

When the pastor spoke to me in a very demeaning manner, it was appalling. I was left with no words to describe my view of him. I lay on the floor, wondering what was going to happen to my baby's lifeless body.

But because my God never sleeps, money for my daughter's proper burial became available just in time. Without the fatherly love of kindness, I honestly don't know what would have come of that unfortunate situation.

Today, I have learned to look at life from a different perspective. I love people—strangers and neighbors alike. For one thing, I have been able to get over what that man of God did to me. I realize just how important it is that I forgive and move on.

And because I didn't want to be hurt twice – once by my daughter's passing and another by the pastor's disrespectful, moronic demeanor, though easily said than done, I had to let go. I have found peace with myself. I had to do it first of all for my daughter and lastly for myself. I had to make myself believe it wasn't his responsibility to help me lay my daughter to rest after all.

Nonprofit

What does "nonprofit" really mean? When I was innocent and naive, I thought "nonprofit" meant "not for profit." What I failed to realize was that every institution—both for-profit and nonprofit organizations—needed money to function at full capacity. I didn't know where money to run nonprofit organizations came from; I just thought they ran on their own without the need for money.

Most, if not all, nonprofit organizations solicit donations from ordinary citizens in order to function. Others accept donated items, which are then sold for profit. Proceeds from the items are then allocated as necessary. The need for such institutions is too great for government entities alone to handle, given the fact that there are people on every street corner of every state who seek some sort of help from these nonprofit organizations.

Homelessness has opened my eyes to the reality of some of these nonprofit organizations.

Many of the places where my kids and I have lived since becoming homeless do, in fact, fall within the category of a nonprofit organization 501(c)(3). These organizations have turned out to be the best places on the planet.

They took us in when no one else could. They gave us a new meaning in life. They were there when nobody else was paying any attention to us. I honestly cannot resist the temptation to wonder what might have come of us had it not been for the help selfless men and women rendered at those very difficult times.

The good, hardworking men and women at these institutions take it as their personal responsibility to ensure every family's needs are met and their dreams realized. All they ask of you is that you follow simple, set rules.

Some people go into these institutions with their own preconceived notions, but one cannot confuse that with being able to follow simple rules designed to keep these places running smoothly.

If women were allowed to do what they saw fit, like being able to bring home their boyfriends as they pleased, these places would be deemed useless. It only makes sense to assume a homeless mother of three would take galvanizing her efforts toward becoming independent in a hurry a prime obligation.

As a single mother, your first priority should be digging for financial freedom rather than looking for yet another image that will only jeopardize your chances at success again.

Most women, myself included, fall in love with an image, which is not necessarily what they so desire. We want something or someone with a broader appeal, but sometimes we fail to realize something that would appeal to me might not have any appeal to you, because our needs and aspirations are completely different. We are different people.

You know yourself better than anyone, and you know what your wants and needs are. People who allow others to show them the way are more inclined to fail than those whose paths are well defined.

The Ups and Downs

"Struggle" would be an understatement for what my kids and I have gone through. When we had no place to call home, I cried because nothing seemed to make any sense. At other times my head went blank as I tried to understand what was happening to us.

There were times when I wanted to speak to someone, but that person appeared more distant than I had ever imagined. The only time I didn't have to overwhelm my brain with thought was when I went to sleep at night. Even then, my dreams were repetitive. I had the same dreams every night.

I wanted something different, although I wasn't quite sure how that change would look like. The dreams and thoughts almost drove me to the limits. But I knew how best to approach life after having gone through so much terror in every corner of life. Staying collective was perhaps my only chance at survival.

Motherhood gave me a reason to believe in myself, to be strong and optimistic, even when nothing seemed possible. I wanted to be a good mother to my children. And at whatever the cost, I was determined to make good on that promise.

Humanity

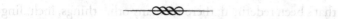

People from all walks of life are trained to think a certain way, in that our brains are programmed to identify activity of different characteristics and make determinations based on what we think we know, whether the underlying factor is, in fact, correct or not. For example, when we see someone who looks nothing like us, we are quick to think something is wrong with that person. The only things that distinguish us from one another are our belief systems and the way we conduct ourselves. What we fail to understand also is that the world is more complete when we learn to welcome others and live peacefully together, regardless of color, religion, and where we come from.

A long time ago, family consisted of a father, a mother, and their children. Today, even this simple fact has been rewritten to accommodate human truths. As the world moves, so do the values! One can only wonder what comes next. We all try to hold on to what we believe to be true, but when time changes, we are left holding on to outdated information that presents nothing of value.

Although we can readily agree that marriage has been redefined, we also can understand the implications brought forth by these changes. And marriage isn't the only thing that's been redefined; there are many other things, including virginity, religion, education, etc. That makes us think not one thing is left to chance.

It doesn't take rocket science to distinguish the difference between movies produced today and those from a century ago. Movies from a long time ago, for instance, were more about family and reality. Today, however, almost every movie being produced is about fantasy and life in space. Remember the numbers game? It's about the numbers. Everything we do in life revolves around those same numbers, usually from zero to nine. If you haven't had time to look at these numbers and understand how important they are, you need to do that now, while you can. These numbers have the power to change not only the world, but everything in it, as well.

Change is everywhere! In the bygones, in some countries, a woman who never married was considered a spinster; one without a child was said to be barren. What does that mean? Quite simply, it means every woman must get married and have children.

When a woman without a child died, she was buried with a piece of charcoal. This was because a long time ago in the village, people believed that a barren woman had the power to come back after death and haunt the whole village.

Now, was that true? Well, what you should know is that this was a belief system many people maintained for ages. It sounds foolish, but I'm quite sure those people had their own genuine reason that made them think that way - culture.

Education and the Misconception

Have you ever wondered why people who are not educated are always looking to employ very well-educated individuals? This is because whoever has the money, the most numbers, controls the game. As human beings we are trained to think or look at things a certain way. We are made to believe rich people are more knowledgeable than those who are not, when in fact there's no truth to that.

The same is true of educated individuals - our society tends to think educated people are wiser than those who are not. People don't seem to realize that education does not change anyone. Someone can have all the degrees in the world and still be stupid.

What about young children with talent? The numbers game is what this is about! Of course, some people learn skills by attending college, while others are born with them. I've seen skilled people with no formal education. And if, in fact, college was that important, why then is it overpriced? You can argue with me here, but that will not change the fact that college has become more about making money than it is about educating people.

My grandfather knew how to predict weather; does that mean he went to school to study weather? Not exactly! It simply means he knew how to identify certain characteristics that made him aware of what to expect that year. If the year in question was going to be without much rain or drought, he knew how to read the sky accordingly and, yes, even the bushes. Scientists, on the other hand, spend years in college studying weather characteristics, when my grandfather learned from observation. Are you still with me? It's all in the numbers!

We are reminded time and again about the importance of education, but people who have the most money are not necessarily the very educated. I know quite a few who are well educated and wise, but they are in the minority. I have also seen very educated people without riches and uneducated super-rich ones. The notion that education is the only way to success is deceiving. It is up to you to keep following the wind. Or find something you can do better than anyone else, and capitalize on that.

If you know how to arrange closets, for example, offer those services for a fee to people who do not have time to arrange their closets. Whatever you know you are good at, offer to do it for other people at a reasonable fee. That will allow you to work, but you will work on your own terms, with no degree. If you want to be a computer scientist, then perhaps you should go to college to study, but that doesn't mean you kiss other people's behinds to survive. Life is a basic right to which every human being is entitled.

It also is important that you know that life isn't supposed to be a struggle. Life is meant to be easy and enjoyable. If you are struggling or working too hard to strike a balance in your life, just know that you are doing something wrong. Stop what you are doing, it probably isn't for you. Look for other avenues.

You must remember that we are all called to do different things for the world to run effectively. If you are doing another person's work, your work will remain untouched until you identify it. Whether you are educated or not, you have a place in this world to which you are entitled.

When I was working on my accounting degree, sometimes I spent three hours on one problem because I refused to use advanced calculators. I refused to use a calculator or any other tool that's available today because I didn't want to be dependent on technical tools. I wanted to use only my brain.

Using tools to get high grades is a form of cheating. And you can disagree with me here, and that's okay. After all, as human beings, we are not designed to agree on everything. A genuine debate is fine. It is the way in which we learn new things. It's okay to even think I'm foolish; I don't have anything to lose besides the fact that I trust my brain.

I worked my butt off to get good grades, but that was before I realized there was nothing to burn my supercharged intelligence for. So I dropped out. I didn't have time to waste on UN calculated myths when I could do better with other things.

Housekeeping

What is it? To me it means keeping your home clean. To others in the hospitality industry, it's about experience. The first thing I did when I obtained my employment authorization was to look for a job that didn't require degrees.

Perhaps most surprising was that even a housekeeping position required a certain level of experience. Once there, I quickly became aware that some of the housekeeping managers didn't know how to construct a sentence in English. Then I thought, *Well, maybe it's because they've been here longer than I have.* Then I thought, *Wait, it's because they're bilingual.* Aside from English, some housekeeping managers spoke other languages that made them more valuable than me. As time went by, I came to realize that my set of skills could make for a better candidate than most people who spoke another language.

It all falls in line with what we've known all along about our deeply centered biases that make some people think they are better than others. We are all unique; we are not duplicates. Every human being is one of a kind, and that one can only be as good or bad as him. And that a situation can only be as good or bad as you think it is. This reiterates just how a human mind can sometimes be corrupt.

When you are in your own little world, you are always made to believe your world is better than everyone's. It's not until you go around the neighborhood before you can actually begin to see why your mentality is not only wrong but fraudulent as well.

Billionaires live the luxuries of life; on the other hand, the poor are constantly playing catch-up. For what? Not a single thing! Life is what you make of it. If you think life is about driving a very expensive car, then that's what it's about. If you think life is about appreciating the little you have, then that's what it's about. Period!

You need to stop emulating others and enjoy your simple life a little bit more, or keep following what is until you lose track of the one thing you have: Your life. We all know that money buys you the luxuries of life but not necessarily happiness. People with lots of money are human beings; people without enough money are also human beings.

This concept will remain true until one day some scientist comes up with another scientific definition that will change everything we have known all along. It's up to you to believe what you want; the truth is clear. Enjoy your simple life. Complicated lives are sometimes too much for humans to take. Keep in mind though that not one person, whether rich or poor, takes with him his possessions when he dies.

Therefore, it is important that we take life for what it is. You can have more than you possibly need to live your life in style, the concept remains the same. Swing or stand on your tiptoes, and struggle to make your ends meet, nothing is out of the ordinary. Life is what it is! I may not fathom the science behind riches, but I know that no one gets rich by working for another.

Growing Up in the Village

In the village, we played jump rope during daytime and hide-and-seek after dark, and sometimes we all sat around a fire and told stories. At other times we sang and danced in a circle. We were left alone to enjoy the innocence of being kids. We didn't have a need to flirt with boys; there really was no reason for us to be in such a hurry.

Today, most people tend to think that somehow in order to be beautiful, you must have a boyfriend at a tender age. Is this true? Maybe not! Our father and mother were in no hurry to introduce any of their children to the outside world. They let us mature before we gained access to too much information. I miss being naive.

Naive is perhaps a good thing; too much of something is toxic. It's one way or the other; you can't have it both ways. We can either choose to teach our children the decency of being kids or allow them to become wildcats. There is no middle ground. This, in other words, could simply mean depriving our children of discipline and innocence.

Hollywood pretty much runs every household across the globe. Where Hollywood goes, so goes the world. Even if it means taking wrong turns, there too, the world will follow, which has been the case in most instances. Some famous people think walking naked is the way to be beautiful, when, in fact, it just shows how desperate and ignorant they are. Then they wonder why their marriages last for only a month.

If you are beautiful, you can wear long dresses and still amaze the world. Nobody wants to see your beautiful body, it's for your husband alone to see. If you think you are beautiful naked, then don't worry about your underwear; walk around naked so the world can see your little you.

Many of us are allowed to do as we please, with little to no accountability of any sort. Our beautiful world, as a result, has been turned into one big pile of garbage, a wasteland. It is fine to emulate people who, despite the nature of their highly demanding, tightly versed jobs, still find a way to strike a balance between the life of a star and that of a normal human being.

As parents, we are in control of what kind of life we choose for our children, or so we think. Honestly, I feel hopeless sometimes... at the amount of garbage to which our children are exposed, day in and day out: The movies, the news, the games, you name it. After which we wonder what's happening to our children! The numbers game! Most people would readily agree that violence and sex do, in fact, sell. Yeah, big bucks! But at what cost? Tally the numbers!

I don't know about you, but I would want my kids to be allowed to be kids, to be naive and innocent. That's what I want for my grandkids too. Can you imagine what it would take to create such an environment for our children? Perhaps not much if it weren't for greed. Creating an environment that allows our kids to be kids could probably be met with too big of a fight; it would probably be the biggest fight Mankind would ever have to fight in this life cycle. It's all in the numbers.

When we do or say certain things to our children, we are declared unfit to parent. Yet movie producers, shows, games, and so on, get away with almost anything. Double standard! It's up to you to do your math correctly.

In real life you can do things only one way or the other. You do it the right way or the wrong way. You can't have both. This decision leaves you a window of opportunity to choose right or left. And remember, there's no middle ground.

The Double Standard

A double standard is when we criticize others for doing the same things we do to satisfy our bad intentions. Somehow, we think it is okay to commit adultery, but when others do it, we disapprove of it.

The same double standard that motivates us to criticize older women for going out with younger men... is the same standard that allows us to assume it's okay for older men on sex advancement drugs to go out with younger women; the standard that wants women to walk around naked, when all men are fully clothed, is the standard intelligent women defy.

Intelligent women know how to protect their bodies. Foolish ones don't. Beautiful women don't have time for married men. A married man is dirty, as is a married woman. We know what happens in those bedrooms when nothing is off limits.

Why can't men be blamed for cheating on their wives? Women are criticized more than men when it comes to cheating. Why? Communities in which we live have deeply centered biases. We tend to think that women are to blame for three-quarters of broken marriages. What we fail to realize is that most men don't tell the truth when they prey on their targets. Some of them even go to the extreme of removing their wedding rings just to hide their pathetic, ill-conceived theories.

The truth is that knowingly going out with a married man or woman is pure evil and stupid. People who do that have no self-worthiness. The world has billions of people; why not find your own? If a man or woman leaves you for another, chances are they will betray you too. Double standards!

The same rings true about dating older men or older women. If a much older man is dating a young lady half his age, people don't seem to care much. But when this concept is in reverse order, the whole world is inclined to pay attention. Double standard!

In most cases, the only logical motive would be money. When men get too old, even Viagra stops working. Why then would one want to marry an elderly person whose sex life is minimal? Those hugs and kisses cannot compensate for a great sexual experience.

My maternal grandfather was a superman in his time. He had six wives, including my mother's mother. In fact, my grandmother was my grandfather's first wife. But because my grandfather's sex drive was too high for my grandmother to live up to, she let him marry another woman and then another and another.

Heard of anything like this before? Regardless of what you think, you need to know that my grandmother loved her husband dearly. She wanted him to be happy; she wasn't a self-serving egomaniac with hidden motives. She loved her husband, with whom she had their first, beautiful child, although my grandfather later had twenty-six of his own and sixty grandchildren.

My grandmother let this happen not because she was stupid or naive, but because she had her own motivations. She would rather have her husband marry more women than have him cheat on her.

I think they had genuine conversations with each other before my grandfather married a second wife? I'm sure they did! And I can honestly tell you that my grandmother and grandfather died happy. Their love for each other was sincere and pure, although it doesn't appear that way to the outside world.

At age seventy-two, my grandfather slept in his own bedroom alone. He had reached retirement age, when he no longer had sexual desires. Grandfather and Grandmother sat around a fire in the kitchen to talk about what was left of them. The two had been together too long because they married young and spent their lives together.

Grandfather loved my siblings and me more than all his grandchildren combined, simply because we were his first wife's offspring.

His wives became more like his sisters than his wives in old age. The younger ones were let go at their own will; my grandfather no longer had any use for them, and Viagra was not something my grandfather saw himself taking. "Sex, I suppose, is meant to be natural," he said. "If I have to take aids to enhance my sex drive, then I don't want it. I'm too old for that," he pleaded.

In some countries, men can marry more than one woman, and that's okay... as long as they have plans for how to accommodate them all. In Western countries, however, that is not even an option.

But time and again, we've seen married men with mistresses. What's the difference? It's all in the numbers. If a man is going out with a woman besides his wife, he's a polygamist. Call it what you may! After all, no one is entitled to his own opinion.

You can paint a pig with many different colors, but it won't change the fact that it's a pig. A pig is a pig! I think most men cheat on their wives one way or another. Don't get me wrong! Women cheat too, but not nearly as much as men do.

Arnold Schwarzenegger would make for a classic example of what I'm talking about here. The entire world heard of that horrible, self-manufactured phenomenon that tore apart a very good family. That, needless to say, was a perfect storm in unfortunate circumstances. I believe the mistress, with whom the disgraced governor had an extramarital child, did not deserve anybody's attention, yet we live on a wasteful, civilized planet where garbage accounts for everything newsworthy or otherwise.

What the governor did is another perfect example of how politicians take things for granted. But, let us not forget there's an innocent wife and children worthy of some privacy here.

The problem though is the way in which the news is presented. When a news crew is invited into one's bedroom, what follows is chaos. If you have a crew of six, by the time the story breaks, you will have twelve fully formulated stories, all geared toward impression with no regard for truth.

People love real stories, which explains why we have gossip shows popping up all over the place. Nothing is wrong with that... except that it's all about celebrities and their dark lives. Nobody says much about poor children who deserve the attention of every human being on earth. We know there are more poor children in the world than there are rich people. Children without proper representation live in the dark shadows of world noises. Why not talk more about them? Um! The numbers for that do not amount to anything, or do they?

The Independent Mind

The human mind has its own way of processing information as it becomes available. Once that information has been processed, the human mind will then make its determination without bias. This is known as independent thinking.

When two or more individuals come together to assess the outcome of a situation, you have what is called a debate. In this debate, you have people whose minds process information differently. If you are not a firm believer in what you already know, you will change your mind quite a few times before you finally settle on the truth. Noises have the ability to distort truth and cloud our judgment. The determination you make before any noises occur is the truth and is usually unbiased.

It is not unusual for people from different parts of the world to think differently. This is because people have different belief systems. For example, in America someone who kills another being is innocent until proven guilty. This perhaps is the problem. In other countries, however, this is just the opposite. If you take a life, no money or law will protect you enough, regardless of the circumstances leading up to the killing, it's considered murder.

Murder is not to be taken lightly; it is satanic to take a life you did not create and try to justify your evil belief. In most cases, murderers claim self-defense. Well, good luck with that! In the end, you will be accountable for your actions. Keep in mind that when that time comes for all humans to face real trial, everything about you, good or bad, will be revealed, leaving you with no room to hide or place to foster your lies.

The Information Age

A long time ago, my father said there was only one way to succeed in life: Go to school, study very hard and bring home the good grades, so you can get a secure job with better pay and benefits. But there's only one problem with this kind of mentality—it's Industrial Age thinking, and we are no longer in the Industrial Age. Many jobs out there today are not good enough to take care of you. This explains why a lot of hardworking people are struggling to make ends meet. We live in a new century, and the rules have changed many times over.

Job security is a thing of the past that carries little to no value. It is also true that Social Security and Medicare will run out of funds in the near future. Before the bubble burst in 2008, many passionately believed their retirement savings were safe. These plans are backed by mutual funds and blue-chip stocks, they were told. Well, that remained true until everything they thought they knew changed, and it did so in an instant. People's life savings were wiped out in a flash.

If you were there when the economy crashed, then you know where I'm coming from. I'm not well educated, because education is costly, but I know what I know. I know enough to know that this is home. Home is where we belong, and we are here to stay.

Every person, regardless of their educational background, deserves to have a good job with better pay. This is not something to debate when there are so many families involved. Maybe by the time I'm done writing this book, unemployment will once again be on the rise. And it's okay to believe what you want. Good jobs with better pay have been replaced with useless ones that don't amount to much of anything. This is why there are more people on public benefits than there ever were.

When the economy falls, the government is left to pick up the tag. Why? Do the math! In my opinion it's bad planning. This kind of planning is what led up to the economic collapse in 2008, affecting almost three-quarters of the world. People who thought they had saved enough were left holding on to nothing. Homes lost half their value. This has come and gone, but the question is: Are you ready for what is to come next?

I have seen jobs offering eighteen to nineteen dollars per hour to educated people with bachelor's degrees, depending on experience. This is an insult to people investing in education with hopes of securing good jobs with better pay.

At the end of the day, people are left with huge student loan debts to pay for the rest of their lives. Besides student loans, most people have mortgages to pay off, too. By the time they are done with their debts, they will be left with nothing else to live for, as they will be too old to enjoy the luxuries of life.

Life for ordinary people across the globe is a gamble. Greed and corruption are at the epic center of the madness.

In the United States of America, minimum wage should be around twenty-three dollars per hour or more... to allow people to live longer. Minimum wage is another form of cancer here to destroy the livelihood of humanity.

People with jobs should not have to depend on public benefits for survival. Without these hardworking people, businesses, big and small, would shut down.

Life in America is expensive; this argument extends far beyond our borders. Rent is between one thousand and fifteen hundred dollars or more, depending on where you live. Add six hundred dollars for food to that, and you inch closer to two thousand dollars. But there are other bills to be paid, such as water, electricity, phone, transportation, school supplies, and cable. After paying all these bills, you are left with nothing to put in your savings account for rainy days. This is what most people would call survival of the fittest!

In developing countries, some people don't work nearly as hard as people in civilized countries; people in developing countries make pennies on a dollar, yet do just fine. Whereas in industrialized world, you have to make in excess of five thousand dollars per month to be comfortable. What's a dollar really worth? When you look at how far a dollar can stretch in some countries, you will begin to realize that it doesn't go far enough.

With every dollar you earn, after taxes, you are left with pennies. These taxes are spent on building infrastructure - roads, bridges, schools, and so on. Great! But why are some so adamant about offering tax cuts? In the end, it's the poor people, people whose numbers don't amount to anything, who pay more in taxes. Do the math.

Life on Opposite Sides
of the Hemisphere

Having lived on opposite sides of the hemisphere has given me much insight. It has propelled my thinking capabilities. I know the difference between good and bad and right and wrong and rich and poor.

While people in developing countries don't earn nearly as much as people in civilized countries, life in developing countries is more easygoing compared to that of civilized countries. For instance, in order to have a comfortable life in civilized countries, one must make in excess of seven thousand dollars per month, whereas in developing countries, one can make less than two thousand dollars and still live comfortably. As a matter of fact, most people in developing countries make less than one thousand dollars a month, yet do just fine. What's the dollar really worth? It's the numbers game!

A dollar is actually worth something, or it wouldn't be the most traded currency in the world. Almost every country accepts the dollar, making it the most powerful and distinguished currency of all time. Therefore, it is too fair of an assumption to say the world runs on the dollar.

When I was a business lady a long time ago, I carried dollar bills to South Africa, Zimbabwe, Kenya, and The United Arab Emirates every time I traveled. They were accepted everywhere, only at different rates. The world runs on the dollar! Why then do people in America have to work so hard to make ends meet?

Colleges, private as well as public are overpriced. Making college expensive allows poverty to indulge itself within the roots of the foundation of a country, leaving people with no other choices from which to choose but depend on the government itself. This speaks to why more people are now looking for ways to start their own businesses with hopes of making more money.

For a reasonable amount of time, I thought homelessness was the result of laziness, stupidity, or bad timing. But after becoming homeless myself, I had to rethink my view of homelessness. My children and I became homeless for reasons contrary to those I've listed here.

I learned to work hard at a very tender age. I didn't really understand the technical ramifications of it, but I knew enough to know that one had to work hard to live like a king, although that too has proved to be wrong.

Even this once typical, politically correct assumption has come to be challenged one way or the other. The work-hard era has come and gone. Today, a new slogan has emerged: "Don't work harder, work smarter." Surprising? Not exactly! It's all in the numbers. A lot of good, hardworking people have fallen victim to the numbers game, myself included. Fairness does not mean a thing anymore.

Raising children on pennies on a dollar is not only tricky but confusing, as well. It's a calculated myth that leads to no good. I don't see how a family of four can depend on two thousand dollars per month. I might not have studied finance in school, but still able to differentiate the difference.

Raising a family on pennies is politically and financially impossible. You can tally your numbers all you want, but you will still come up short.

Writing for money came at a hefty price for me. I didn't go to school to shell out money I didn't have, but I waited until I almost lost my life before I began to examine what options were available to me. When I realized some people were savages, I had to figure out how to make money with no investment. And the only option I kept rubbing shoulders with was writing. Don't get me wrong. I once was an inept writer.

There are tons of Ponzi schemes out there, taking advantage of struggling people; stone-cold thugs with no regard for life will stop at nothing from snatching out of your hands your very last dollar.

The only investment you will ever have to make with writing is knowing where and how to place those words to create a logical pattern. You can go to school to learn to write, but you will still need your own skills and determination to make your work stand out. Writing can sometimes be a pain in the ass, too.

No teacher on the planet will teach you everything you need to know about writing. Certain things are developed, not learned. No one goes to school to learn a talent; instead, people go to school to learn how to enhance the talent they already possess. If you are like me, with no money saved, then you don't have to wait until you have a burning desire for money or you have a near-death experience to open your eyes.

Writing comes naturally to me, and I only write when I have the stomach for it. I was born with my writing skills.

There are times when I have to interrupt my sweet dreams to jot down important thoughts before they are gone forever. If you are like me, then you know what I'm trying to explain here.

It doesn't make any sense for a blind person to lead the way for another. Listening to get-rich-quick schemes that populate the Internet is like following a blind person: *do what I say, not what I do.*

At times I just look and laugh out loud at the Internet madness. "I found software that prints dollars," so they say. In no time, thousands line up just to get spoofed. From there, they store my money, they say. Once their money is gone, where is the government? The government is exactly where you left it yesterday when you decided to go hiking.

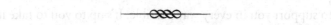

Life in Exile

Shelters provide a family-like environment to homeless families. The setting allows people—in most cases, women and their children—to start over. Single mothers are given reason to believe they too are actually worth something.

Such help couldn't have come at a more critical time to us – me and my children, at a time when my kids and I needed it most. Objectively, I thought no one would care about our well-being. Homelessness comes at a very high price from which most people never recover. In order to make it out in one piece, I learned to prioritize my goals. I kept a very close eye on my mental health. Without it you are done. You become yet another casualty of greed and power mongering.

Having a roof over our heads was one goal I had in mind, and I knew that to be able to do that I was going to have to build relationships with people in charge of these places. That was the best I could do. I noticed, however, that some people wanted to take the highway, which to me seemed like just another miscalculated diversion. Given the volatility of the situation, the best I could do was to remain collective as I tried to recover from my past experiences.

The wonderful men and women at these places are there to support you in every way possible. It's up to you to take it or leave it. And I know that people are quick to find faults than appreciate the simplicity of having a roof over their heads.

Choice become far more distant than it had ever appeared. In other words, choice was a luxury neither my kids nor I could afford. The situation in which we were yielded not too many results. But, rather than disagree on things I didn't like, I let the situation work itself out.

Unlike the shelter in Kansas City, MO, in Los Angeles, CA we were entitled to receiving visitors, limited to a few hours every once in a while. At both shelters we had assigned laundry schedules by which to abide. We also had rotating chores lists. If you cleaned the hallways last week, for example, then you would clean the laundry room next.

I met very well-educated, beautiful beings, most of whom did not deserve to be there. Each had a tall tale to narrate. I was more interested in becoming self-sufficient and quickly moving on with life. But even this very simple, easily calculated analysis, would somehow hit unexpected roadblocks here and there.

I went without a job for a few months, and that meant no savings for me. The more I stayed home, the more I realized just how big of a deal it was to be homeless. We weren't allowed to have TVs in our apartments. This is how their system is set up. It isn't complicated to understand the importance of news. So I bought a small, affordable TV, one that could receive only the local news, as cable was not a possibility. It was not allowed.

Speaking out if I didn't like something was something I didn't want to let go of. As homeless and hopeless as I had become, I wasn't afraid to speak my mind.

Of course, I was very aware of my situation, but I was not about to give up my rights. Human rights are the basic principles upon which every person exists.

After all, life isn't supposed to be complicated, for it is the basic right to which we are all entitled as human beings. I can't resist thinking there's enough money in this world to care for every person regardless of their ability to make money. Yet even this straightforward, commonsense algorithm has time and time again been tested. It has become a game of chance to many who spend more time struggling and none living.

The Speech

I was given the opportunity to speak when our donors came to visit Family Housing in Los Angeles, CA. The first speech follows:

> Good morning. My name is Viora, and welcome to family housing.
>
> When my kids and I left Atlanta, we left behind everything we loved and cherished: friends, coworkers, jobs, schools, and neighborhoods, to which were accustomed. But leaving Atlanta was a decision I had to make if I were to live old enough to see my grandkids.
>
> I didn't know how to begin to navigate the fact that my kids and I were about to become homeless. Relocating to California without a plan or money to keep us afloat was like climbing Mount Kilimanjaro without proper hiking gear.
>
> There's no right way to describe homelessness. The magnitude of its impact is indescribable. It brings with it unexpected turns, unwanted changes,

and unintended circumstances, but such is life. I have learned to keep at heart the simple fact that life cannot be taken for granted.

These shelters turned out to be the best places on earth, where manna still falls from the sky above us. Family housing has given us hope. It has given us the tools necessary for our success: Counseling for me and my kids, tutoring for my kids, domestic violence classes, all of which are offered at no cost to families. Also, 60 percent of items in my credit file have been deleted. My pocketbook is heavier than it's ever been.

It's not rocket science to realize that our bodies are built for happiness and joy, and even as I reflect on what my kids and I went through before leaving home, I never forget to put on a smiley face every single day.

I will take with me life's lessons only the wondrous place can offer. I will be able to pursue my writing degree, thanks to the wonderful men and women who made that a reality. When my kids and I live here, we will live one happy family and with all the necessary tools geared toward our success. And it is for that simple fact I will forever be thankful to wonderful men and women, and to all of you who took a minute out of your fully occupied schedules to come and visit us. Thank you!

A week or two after giving this speech to our sponsors, I was again approached to speak at a Christmas party. I thought it was a pleasure to be able to speak in front of people with different backgrounds. I write for money, not to impress, particularly. Either way I took the invitation as a blessing. And so it goes:

Good evening, and welcome home.

When my kids and I left Atlanta, we left behind everything we loved and cherished: friends, coworkers, good jobs, schools, and neighborhoods, to which were accustomed. But leaving Atlanta was a decision I had to make if I were to live old enough to see my grandkids grow up.

I didn't know how to begin to navigate the fact that my kids and I were about to become homeless. Relocating to California without a plan or money to keep us afloat was like climbing Mount Kilimanjaro without proper hiking gear.

Moving from one place to another, and then another, and another, has since become commonplace for me and my kids. It's become the new norm, so to speak.

While there are things we wish should have stayed the same or lasted forever, we must also believe that in the world in which we live, change is inevitable. And sometimes we labor more than usual to keep up with the pace at which change occurs. It is about time we begin to realize that sometimes change is about just all we need in order to break the cycle—the cycle of struggle, domestic violence, humiliation, homelessness, and poverty.

Please know that comfort feels good, but sometimes it is the same comfort that prohibits us from reaching our highest potential. I don't see how I could get comfortable if all my needs are yet to be met: Having a good job with better pay, a big house, fancy cars, a good neighborhood, and a better education for my kids. You must, therefore, understand that life is just as good or bad as you think it is, and that a human being can be only as good or bad as himself.

This holiday season you owe it to yourself, your kids, and your neighbors to be the best that you can. Life is too short to spend it calculating your life's savings. With that in mind, we must then begin to fathom that certain things matter more than others: Good health, strength, mental health, thinking ability and capacity, and so on.

Please understand that I was given the opportunity to converse on a topic of my choosing. Of course, I could have humbly chosen to speak about money, for it is the root cause of most of our problems here, but instead I chose to share words of encouragement, because the holiday season does not allow for a financial lecture. It is a time in which we share, encourage one another, and respectfully reflect on past occurrences.

Even as we celebrate this holiday season, let us not forget the wonderful men and women who have worked tirelessly to make many dreams come true, and all the selfless men and women and all of our sponsors, who have taken it as their personal responsibility to see to it that every family's holiday here at the center of hope is one to remember.

Please allow me to simply say thank you from the deepest wells of my soul. Thank you!

Homelessness has allowed me to appreciate things that really matter in life: good health, mental capacity, and stability. Before I was homeless, I viewed people who were in this same category... differently. I thought most people became homeless by choice—for example, drug addicts and alcoholics. These groups of people do, in fact, have a choice to make; drugs and alcoholism are a matter of life and death.

When I became homeless, I began to realize there were just as many reasons as there were people who were homeless, each with completely different circumstances.

Homelessness affects all of us in one way or the other. We contribute to the well-being of every person by paying taxes, whether or not we are eligible for benefits ourselves. We must therefore realize that homelessness is everyone's problem, not just for a select few.

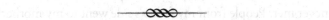

Cultural Kidnapping

In the village there's what is known as cultural kidnapping (*kulobosha* in ILA, father's dialect). What if Mother did not alert me to what the elders in the village had been planning for months? Well, a group of strong men would have muzzled me while I slept and delivered me to the man in question, where I would have probably spent a few nights with his family—mother, father, sisters, brothers, and so on. After getting comfortable, I would then be introduced to my husband for the first time.

You must by now be wondering, *What in the world?* Yeah, me too! I too wonder, *What in the world?* when people utilize dating sites to find dates. The only distinction between online dating and cultural kidnapping is that with cultural kidnapping, parents from both sides agree. Online dating site users take a bet by putting their trust in complete strangers.

Therefore, it is important to know that there are many cultures around the world, most of which are completely different from the one to which we are accustomed.

Whatever your belief system, there always will be people questioning your method, and that's okay too.

When my father proposed to my mother, the two had never met. People from my father's side went to my mother's to propose. And it wasn't my mother's decision to make. Her father called the shots.

My grandfather asked for fifteen cattle without first asking my mother if, in fact, she wanted to get married to my father. This was how their belief system worked. Perhaps you need to know that most of these old-fashioned marriages lasted forever.

Most women in Mother's time were full-time housewives, and most of their husbands were heads of the households. Women stayed home to clean, cook, wash clothes, draw drinking water, fetch firewood, have children, and etc. Their husbands worked hard to provide for their families. This perception is one that has held its own for ages.

There were times when my father had to go to work in Salisbury in neighboring Zimbabwe, and was gone for months at a time. When mother ran out of food or money before Father came home, my maternal grandfather was always there to ensure our family had everything needed.

Our grandfather gave us all the love we ever wanted. When we went to his farm on school holidays, we slept with him in the same bedroom. I wondered when and how he had sex with all those women he had lined up. He told us that he wanted to spend as much time with us as he possibly could. He also reminded us that we were only passing by.

When I was a young girl I was very inquisitive, as are most children. I was eager to know things, hence, asked a lot of questions. Our grandfather was not afraid to candidly answer every question we had, including questions about his love life. Nothing was out of bounds with Grandfather.

I remember asking him how he divided his love among six wives. First, he laughed as stared into space. He then asked me to sit down next to him and said, "listen, every human being is unique, and no two people are the same." He went on to tell me that none of his wives were the same and that he loved each of them in a different way.

However, Grandfather admittedly told me that bias was indeed commonplace. "It is not unusual for a man to favor one woman over others, but each one of them does, in fact, have a special place in my heart," he said. "Besides, I do, however, have the ability to gauge each woman's thinking capacity," he added.

As complex and varied as having six wives might seem at first, everything actually falls in place rather quickly. The most difficult, and perhaps the hardest part is building a foundation and principles upon which your marriage is bound. No matter how complicated having six wives may appear to the outside world, all marriages are built on a basic outline.

Besides having to divide his attention among six wives, Grandfather was also responsible for their well-being. He cared for and loved all his wives as only he could. And because we were his first grandchildren, all his wives loved us too. We were the first grandchildren because our mother's mother was Grandfather's first wife, and our mother was their first child together.

When time came for my older brother to marry, it was our grandfather's cattle that had to be exchanged. Our father contributed money, yet others contributed maize and gifts.

In the village when a son comes of age and is ready to marry, it is everyone's business. Uncles, aunts, grandfathers, and so on, come together to contribute whatever they can afford. Others contribute dishes if they don't have cattle or money, as a show of support and togetherness. And this is something they've been practicing for ages. It's a traditional belief system.

Hindsight

Oftentimes we find ourselves blazing through life as though somehow we will be able to go back in time and fix whatever we didn't get right. I wish that were the case, but unfortunately, a journey through life is realistically with a one-way ticket. Therefore, we ought to pass through it knowing a chance to make it right hardly ever comes—not in this life but perhaps the next.

If going back in time were possible, I would have gone back to being a child, when I enjoyed the innocence and naive. Or perhaps I could have married the young man my dearly beloved father wanted me to marry. Perhaps things wouldn't have turned out to be as bad as I thought they would.

The other reason that would have made me want to go back in time is the death of my little girl, Thelma. I have made great strides since her passing, but I don't think I will ever get over losing her that early.

I have tried to fill the void she left behind with pretense. I don't think I've filled it just yet. I find comfort in making myself believe someday we'll meet again.

Destination Is Key

Where a journey begins carries no meaning, destination is key. Where we end up in life matters more than where a life's journey begins. Of course, surprises are to be expected along the way, but even more so when you don't have a strong foundation upon which to rely.

Quite often, we focus on what other people might think of us. What we fail to realize is that people will always give their opinion of others, whether good or bad. And that's life! If you know what you want in life, no amount of noise will be loud enough to distract you from reaching your destination on time.

Therefore, we must understand that certain things will not always go in our favor, and that life can approach us from many different directions, most likely from directions we least expect it. As long as we don't settle for less, we should be okay.

I've been out there for a while now, and nothing feels nearly as good as comfort. But oftentimes it is the same comfort that keeps us from the need. I don't see how I could get comfortable when all of my dreams are yet to be realized.

Somehow it is the final stretch to every destination that is usually the hardest, when you can almost see the finish line. Have you ever wondered why? The answer is simple: because that's when anything can happen, and things can go either way. And that's where your ability to push harder to make it across the finish line comes into play.

If you can't run, walk. If you can't walk, crawl to cross the finish line. The game is not over until it's over. You must cross the finish line by any means necessary. Your determination is the distinction between success and failure.

Industrial America

By the end of the Civil War, America was a society that barely resembled the one today. The commonplace fundamentals of existence were nothing compared to those of today. Almost all the things that contribute to a great nation, were, to some extent, still solid. Political gambling of forcing people out of their comfort while they squeeze them with economic sanctions and also political problems, had yet to appear.

The America of those days was one without telephones, transcontinental railroads, wireless cable, skyscrapers, automobiles, electric lights, trolley cars, million-dollar hotels, or the other luxuries and comforts that the modern-day era supply. The American civilization had not yet begun.

Cities of those days contained unpaved streets, unsewered toilets, and streets with flickering gaslights, but that seemed appropriate at the time. Their unheated coaches, wooden bridges, kerosene lamps, and the rough political methods all explain the changes that have taken place in the past fifty years.

For the most part the language of today is one our grandfathers' grandfathers could not have comprehended. This shows how far the evolution of man and civilization has come. The "trust" had not become common and, therefore, could not be misused. Those were times when everyone's well-being was everyone's business. Greed and corruption had not emerged.

In those days family was the most important thing. Man was still in charge of his family's well-being. Today, however, it all depends on what you want to believe. Nobody knows what family means anymore. One can only imagine how far off the tracks mankind is willing to go in the name of change.

Printed in the United States
By Bookmasters